Flying
Scale
Gliders

Other books in this series include:

Installing Radio Control Aircraft Equipment   Peter Smoothy
Setting Up Radio Control Helicopters   Dave Day
Building from Plans   David Boddington
Basic Radio Control Flying   David Boddington
Operating Radio Control Engines   Brian Winch and David Boddington
Moulding and Glassfibre Techniques   Peter Holland
Covering Model Aircraft   Ian Peacock

Flying
Scale
Gliders

Charles Gardiner

ARGUS BOOKS

Argus Books
Wolsey House
Wolsey Road
Hemel Hempstead
Hertfordshire HP2 4SS

First Published by Argus Books 1989

© Charles Gardiner 1989

ISBN 0 85242 982 7

Phototypesetting by Ethnographica, London N7
Printed and bound in Great Britain by
William Clowes Ltd, Beccles

Contents

Introduction
Why go scale?

Everyone that I have ever spoken to who flies gliders professes to enjoy it—and why not? The glider or sailplane is an excellent flying machine and flying machines are what they are. The description 'model' aircraft is really a misnomer. A model is a miniature of the real thing but a polyhedral or low aspect ratio aerobatic job hardly qualifies as a model. So why do so many kits and designs in this category feature a canopy —or at least a line or painted impression? Perhaps because we are all purists at heart.

Mixture of scale sailplanes, some 1930s, some contemporary: all satisfying.

P.S.S. SE5a from a
Flair Kit, by Phil
Sirs, is a delightful
performer.

John Hill's Dash 7
below is an
example of a multi-
engined prototype
used as a power
scale soarer.

The P.S.S. paddock at a "social meeting" at Clwyd.

Regardless of the purpose for which the model is built, the cockpit is enhanced as a major design feature and appears to be as important as eyes in a face . . . So if aesthetic design marks a cockpit as important, why stop there? It need be no more taxing to produce a flying model of a real aircraft and the satisfaction will fully justify your efforts. There are literally thousands of full-size aircraft suitable for modelling as gliders: the inspiration starts here . . .

No book will tell you all about the subject; this one sets out to give you a look at what's going on in silent flight today and hopefully inspire you to get involved in this most satisfactory and challenging aspect of radio controlled model flight. It is not intended to be a high tech review or definitive book on the subject, just a clubman's eye view to fire your enthusiasm and get you going .

That most scale activity takes place on the slope need not preclude modellers from the flat lands from enjoying scale. Launch from tow line, winch or aerotow and enjoy the fun. The now internationally accepted classification "P.S.S." (power

scale soarers) indicates gliding models of aircraft originally powered by piston, jet or rocket engines. Select your project carefully and you are in business no matter where you fly.

Most scale models make super efficient soarers and the effortless climb away on a centred thermal has to be experienced to be appreciated. If you must use an engine—well, O.K., you can still learn a lot from the glider guiders. Most high-tech developments in airfoils and construction techniques originate from the needs of the contest flier and will eventually be accepted as normal to us mere mortals. But P.S.S. and scale enjoyment need not depend on special materials or skills. Traditional methods still reign supreme—just keep an eye open and an open mind. Have no preconceived ideas and your enjoyment will expand as the scope widens.

There is a whole world of action out there. Build from a kit or plan, research and design from scratch—it doesn't matter what you do as long as you enjoy it. And you will . . .

Chapter 1
What to choose

'What' largely depends on 'where'. The design requirements for satisfactory flying are decided by your site. From a flat field or shallow slope, there is no substitute for wing area. Fly from a steep ridge in good lift and your choice is wide open.

Wing loadings are important (that is, providing your model has a wing) and as most post-1950 jet fighter aircraft are supersonic, the choice in that direction is narrowed somewhat. That still leaves a vast selection of aircraft and sailplanes to model so let's look at the scope.

Undercamber can be seen on this shot of a full-size *Grunau Baby*. **Looks like film!**

Full-size *Gull* is an example of fabric-covered rib-on-spar wing construction.

Gliders and sailplanes can be classified as vintage, post-vintage and glass. The advent of g.r.p. construction and progress in aerodynamics has changed the face of full-size sailplanes and many techniques have worked their way through to the model field.

Vintage gliders typically are rather 'draggy' and the demands made on airframes using materials of the day necessitated external bracing struts and wires. Lower flying speeds dictated larger control surfaces but whatever the problems, their character was undeniable. This class of gliders of course bears a closer relationship to traditional modelling technique, with formers and longerons, ribs and spars. This is real modelling and although many are produced as 'museum pieces', there is no reason why such craft could not be produced in sheet balsa and foam veneer. Illusion is the name of the game and we will come back to that later.

The more modern built-up craft were getting quite sophisticated by the late forties and early fifties. Attention to detail, designing out drag and construction of complex three dimensioned curves brought its own rewards. The development of g.r.p, in addition to facilitating manufacture and drag savings, enabled improvements in weight reduction and distribution, higher aspect ratios, new section development and, just as important, superb accuracy and surface finish.

That modern craft are of g.r.p. construction need not prevent their being modelled using traditional materials. A one-off multi-curved fuselage can be produced more easily in balsa, either carved or planked, so the choice is up to you. Such a model can be flown from the

An *ASW 17* by Vic Grist, an excellent 'glass' ship.

slope or from the flat which extends the attraction of this class—let's have a look at the P.S.S. alternatives.

Pre-1930-ish aircraft were very much of the open cockpit, wire and string rigged variety which, with fixed undercarriages, magnified the dreaded drag factor. Such a model will fly well in moderate wind strengths but will require a disproportionate amount of lead to ensure forward movement in a strong blow.

Pre-war aircraft were a mixed bunch. Biplanes and external rigging still persisted into the forties with Gladiators and Swordfish etc., in contrast to Spitfires and Hurricanes which came in the late thirties, and such delightful aeroplanes as the DC3, which first flew around 1935 and is still in use today in many parts of the world. Here it is opportune to mention that the C47, as the military version of the DC3 was known, also saw limited service as a troop-carrying glider. These were not fitted with engines so although strictly not P.S.S., nevertheless come within the scope of scale gliders along with the Horsas, Hotspurs and Hamilcars etc. of the era.

Although such aircraft were flying faster, they all had one need, that of wing area. The proportions lend themselves well to modelling projects, and they will fly from flat field or shallow slope.

Many piston aircraft from World War II have the attractions of 'model' proportion wing areas but engine weights frequently enforced a shortish nose moment. Central or wing mounted jet engines swung the pendulum the other way and this, together with sweep-back, extended the nose and thus made the modellers' choice much wider.

That is of course until the world went

This miscellaneous selection of
P.S.S. subjects includes a *Piper
Cub*, war-time *DFS* troop-carrying
glider, Swiss-marked *Vixen* and a
Skyraider—quite an assortment and
all fairly small.

supersonic. Without recourse to stretching designs considerably out of scale, it is difficult to select a prototype that will fly in anything but excellent lift. Mind you, the exhilaration of such a model has to be experienced.

Modern subsonic aircraft, however, must rate highly among the all-round scale model aeroplane. Load and passenger carrying aircraft invariably have the right proportions for our purpose so take a look around; you will be amazed at the choice.

That P.S.S. includes rocket-powered craft is no accident. World War II aircraft included the Messerschmitt Me 163 flying wing and the Japanese Kamikaze "Ohka", right through to the Bell X series research aircraft. The V1 flying bomb was in fact a ram jet—so what, fly it!

The growth of P.S.S. has been tremendous over the past few years. Perhaps the time will come when the old-style unimaginative flying machine will be extinct?

Time to decide/Sources of information

"Beauty is in the eye of the beholder" they say. You may also say "there's no accounting for taste". Whatever it is, there are some aircraft that have that certain something which cannot be quantified. The Percival Mew Gull was such a craft, its bigger brother, the Proctor, was the first to lift my carcase from the face of this planet—maybe some day . . .

No doubt some particular glider or aircraft has endeared itself to you over the years and having satisfied yourself on its proportions and where it will have to be flown, you should start to build up a

Ray Jones examines Graham Moodie's version of the *Aermacchi MB 339*

No embellishments on this *Harrier* by **R.M. Green** but you can almost imagine it hovering! Opposite page, sailplane proportions evidenced by the *Tupolev Bear* and the *U2*. But the kamikaze *Ohka* would need stretching. Scale flight pattern not too good!

data base. Keep your eyes open, though, for like many a P.S.S. modeller, you may find that something else will suggest itself as an alternative project.

Make your first stop the plastic kit collection at the local toy or hobby shop. There are a number of manufacturers who seem to have covered most of the interesting aircraft that have ever been produced. If your personal preference is there, so much the better, for you have ready access to an accurate three-view drawing, colour scheme and decals.

Though we have yet to come across plastic kits of gliders and sailplanes, the information contained in a 1/72 (or larger) plastic kit can in fact be adequate for your P.S.S. needs.

Twelve-foot *Lancaster* built largely from paper by Australian Gordon Mackenzie.

Availability of a full-size prototype is the surest way of getting everything accurate. Robbie Bridson's beautiful *Gull* is a faithful reproduction of the full-size machine opposite, also shown in flight on page 10.

The purists may choose to take research further, and the first stop must be the local library where the aircraft section should contain the internationally recognised Janes series of "All the World's Aircraft", "All the World's Sailplanes", and various books detailing particular aircraft, also documentary works on their operation and use. There are specialist book shops who will welcome your enquiries though we suggest that you do not make your browsing too obvious.

The many aircraft museums in this country will be happy to provide information, answer your questions and allow you to photograph the aircraft of your choice including the cockpit and instrument panel details. Don't forget to say "Please".

Full-size aviation magazines carry sufficient details to model many current and historical aircraft but do not forget the information offered by the A.S.P. Plans Service and, in particular, the series which ran for many years in the Aeromodeller on 1/72 full-size aircraft, which carried invaluable information and are still available as reprints. *(The Plans Service is part of the same group as Argus Books and can be reached at the same address).*

Remember, too, that your friends and/or clubmates may possess or have access to the information you need, so don't hesitate to tell people what you have in mind.

Dare I mention too that there are many engine-powered kits of scale models which with modification will make excellent P.S.S. models? Many manufacturers are wakening up to this possibility.

Information on sailplanes is not difficult to obtain. Decide your craft and consult the British Gliding Association, the Vintage Gliding Club or, in America, the Vintage Sailplane Club or Soaring Society of America, who will be pleased to put you in touch with owners of the aircraft in which you are interested. Be careful, though, for these folks have an enthusiasm that is highly contagious! Attend a flying session to seek photographs and information and you are likely to be roped in for rigging and ground handling etc.—but you will certainly be made welcome. Just tell them what you are after.

Research, Documentation, Photography

By now, the aircraft you wish to model should be clear and it is time to build up a profile for your documentation. Ideally, you will need

A three-view drawing,
Photographs to confirm colour and markings,
Detail photographs to verify working features,
Manufacturers' brochures etc.

The last is easier with sailplane and glider manufacturers but research will almost certainly turn up sufficient gen on the P.S.S. prototype of your choice.

At this stage, take the trouble to make yourself a neat folder which includes the necessary information to convey evidence of the original to any judges you may meet along the way. It is impossible to take too many photographs or have too

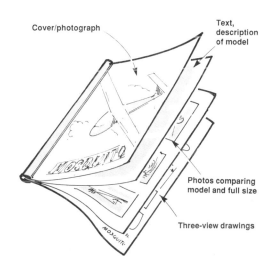

Fig. 1 Assemble your material in a folder.

much information, just don't put it all in the documentation pack.

Worth mentioning at this stage is the need to photograph any insignia and the control panel. Section II gives more information on this but it is helpful to know the effects of distance on your lens and consequent enlargement of a shot. From a distance of four feet, my 50mm lens gives an 'en' print shot that is perfect for a quarter scale insignia etc.

The photographs adjacent are typical of the sort of thing you need; the glider in this instance is the Glasflugel 15m 'Mosquito B' based at the Lancs and Derbyshire Gliding Club at Hucklow. Put that amount of detail onto your model and you will have a winner.

Photos show details of the Glasflugel glider mentioned opposite.

GLASFLÜGEL

mosquito b

Simon Cocker and Ray Jones produced these B52s (see opposite).

Size

From the first principles, the model needs to be big enough to house the radio gear and have sufficient wing area to carry it. Modern miniature radio gear does make the task easier. If you want to use it, fine—but we do not need the extra expense, that is of course unless you specifically wish to create a mini model.

One in Ten

Unfortunately, there has been no attempt yet to "standardise" on any scale for P.S.S. Regardless of the size of the original, we seem to be looking at around four or five hundred square inches of wing area with a loading of some fifteen or twenty ounces per square foot as a higher limit. With this as the optimum slope soarer size, the scale

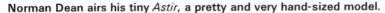

Norman Dean airs his tiny *Astir*, a pretty and very hand-sized model.

Hardly a single-handed launch! Crew needed for Simon Cocker's B52 handling.

needed to bring the full size to this can vary from ¼th for a 48in. span Ohka to 1/32nd for 78in. span B52. The Ray Jones/Simon Cocker B52s are around 1/16th scale but 1/10th may in fact be the optimum and the key to a standardised scale. Some typical examples would be

Lancaster	122in. span
Spitfire	44in. span
Junkers 87D (Stuka)	54in. span
Bell Airacobra	41in. span
ME 262	49in. span
Meteor	50in. span

One tenth gives the average fighter aircraft sufficient area while not pushing the typical World War II bomber too high in span.

Of course, if you must build B52s, Galaxies and the like, then 1/20th should suffice, but why go "over the

Rob Waddington and his ⅓ size T21 at Bosley. Scale effect in flight is magical.

Peter Waller with his *Hercules* which is amazingly realistic in flight.

top"? Such a size strains the building resources, the finances and the muscles, and runs the risk of discouraging newcomers.

Why one in four?

The parameters for area and wing loading are just as applicable to models of scale gliders, but to take a 15m craft

Coming in all sizes are *Hawks*—note the miniature one on the wing of the model in the left-hand picture and the super-size one by Fred Jackson.

Another of Peter Waller's P.S.S. models, this time a Convair B36.

down to 1/10th scale would produce 59in. span and a typical mean chord of some 3.5 inches. Big enough to accommodate the gear, maybe, but desperately short of wing area.

We all appreciate the grace of a quarter-scaler but there has been a noticeable trend to sixth scale or less. Before we go much further, why not settle on one in five — and stick to it? A scale of 1/5th brings a quarter-scale 15m model down from 148in. to 118in., only 30in. maybe but consider the typical differences. A fuselage depth and width at cockpit of 8in. and 6in. becomes 6½in. and 5in. Fuselage length from 60in. to 48in. Weight and wing loadings down from 10lbs and 18 ounces per square foot to 6lbs and 14 ounces. The cost is down in proportion, full size servos can still be used and at this scale, as much detail as necessary can be added.

The 2p coin on the wing of this MB339 indicates that it is fairly small: the coin has a diameter of 1 inch (25mm).

The scale effect is perhaps of less importance. We said that there is no substitute for wing area but how big do you need to go? My admiration for the super size model is unquestioned, but if it should be necessary to build this size to win a contest, then the movement could well collapse.

One thing to remember is that the Civil Aviation Authority (CAA) do have responsibility for air use and it is necessary to obtain an exemption certificate from the Air Navigation Order where the model weight exceeds 5kg (*15kg). See appendix.

Chapter 2
Scale—the philosophy

No model is going to be perfectly to scale. The proportions and materials of construction dictate that the model builder is going to take short cuts and use techniques not available to the full-size aircraft builder.

In appearance, there is not a lot of difference between a glassed, foam veneer wing and a glass sailplane wing, but built-up construction aircraft are a different breed altogether. Our biggest enemy is time—how nice it would be to justify the perfect museum piece—but our objects are satisfaction and, not least, stick time. Acceptable short cuts are therefore essential in our craft.

Full marks to the builder who constructs his model with panels reproducing

Modern sailplanes such as this fine *DG300* model have very different aerofoil sections.

the joint lines of the original. Just as good, however, is a panel line drawn on, for the name of the art is 'illusion'. Illusion means that the model must appear to reproduce full-size construction markings. Whichever means you choose to create this is acceptable to your judges and critics.

Wing sections

The choices for P.S.S. are fairly easy. The fighter type of aircraft which is expected to have an aerobatic ability will benefit from the Eppler 374 range. For anything else, the Eppler 193 will provide soaring and penetrating ability at something akin to a scale flying speed. For construction purposes, the slight undercamber towards the rear of this section can be omitted and the wing built flat on the board. For this class of aircraft, you'll not notice the difference!

On some aircraft the airfoil may be visibly thicker, particularly at the wing root which will be self-evident when drawing up plans. Your discretion will be necessary at this stage, and useful profiles are available in the Clark Y and similar ranges of sections.

Most tailplanes can be a simple 8/10% symmetrical section. No great demands here.

Scale sailplanes are a different breed, however. Typical full size sections are those by Wortman characterised and readily distinguishable by a high under-camber towards the rear of the airfoil. These sections generally work quite well at 1/5th and 1/4th model sizes and they are not too difficult to construct; any deviation from the original will be obvious and unnecessary.

Construction methods

Many traditional methods have been superseded over the past ten years, though longerons, formers and stringers are still used with planking and ply for

Reiher **by Roy Cox at ¼ scale. Flies well in light lift to which aerofoil is suited.** .

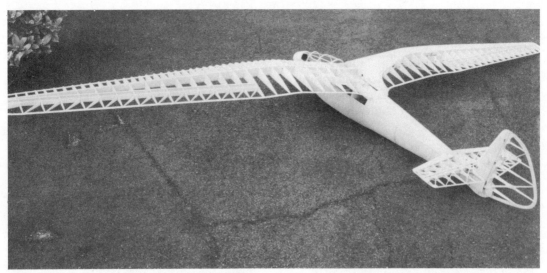

Construction detail of the Bridson *Gull* shows full rib count and ply sectional fuselage.

vintage craft whilst g.r.p. has followed full-size developments for model use. The need to produce a "plug" or model from which the mould is to be made is a time-consuming activity and is only justified where a production run is envisaged.

Now well established in P.S.S. models, particularly where fuselage bulk presents a problem, is construction using foam, either expanded polystyrene or styrofoam (blue foam). This is skinned using veneer, balsa planking or glass cloth and epoxy. Load bearing members of ply or spruce with longerons of balsa form the basic structure as shown in the diagram. Into the spaces are fitted blocks of foam which can then be hot wire cut, one at a time, to the outside shape of the fuselage. Each block is then removed and a further pair of templates used to hollow out the shell, making in effect a skin of say ½ to ¾in. thick.

With larger models, the inside skin is frequently veneered, though for our average lightweight it would be sufficient to veneer on the outside only. Do remember to sand the veneer before sticking it in place, as any attempt

afterwards will simply "lift" the area along formers and longerons which will be unsightly. One advantage of P.S.S. models is that the fuselages are invariably wide enough to be rigid and of adequate strength without need to resort to excessive reinforcement at the rear. Yes, it may break if you pile it in, but then what wouldn't? Add lightness, reduce mass, add strength.

Glass and epoxy is favoured as a covering method but film is used with success, though most aircraft will demand a matt finish for authenticity. Rubbing film with wire wool before covering can suffice to take off the high gloss, but don't overdo it.

Now, dare I suggest that this type of construction may also be used for production of a vintage glider? Simply produce a fuselage from formers, longerons and foam as before, then glue on external stringers of balsa. Cover using a fabric heat shrink material and the judges won't know the difference.

The same applies to other vintage model structures. Cut foam panels, inset spars, wing joiners and any control runs before sticking on the outside what

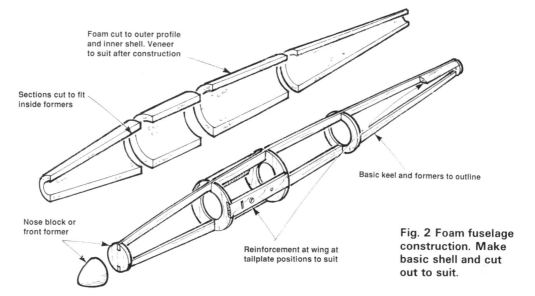

Foam cut to outer profile and inner shell. Veneer to suit after construction

Sections cut to fit inside formers

Basic keel and formers to outline

Nose block or front former

Reinforcement at wing at tailplate positions to suit

Fig. 2 Foam fuselage construction. Make basic shell and cut out to suit.

would appear to be, say, rib capping strips at the appropriate places on the upper surface. Who's going to look underneath? Heat-shrink fabric with a solid or opaque colour and there you have a pretty, quick construction. Same with tailplane and rudder and you could really be classed as a heretic. This is fine, of course, until someone asks for a posed shot of daylight through the covering, but hardly important, for any judge will be looking down on the model, won't he?

Stringers, cap strips or riblets on foam can also give some superb impressions for P.S.S. models too. Imagine a Wellington with full geodetic structure —just under the covering? A similar effect for such a panel lines can be achieved by sticking cotton or thread in place to represent panel lines etc. Providing the spars are adequate, it is acknowledged that blue foam/glass/ epoxy is sufficient without a veneer or balsa skin—and we do need to keep the weight down.

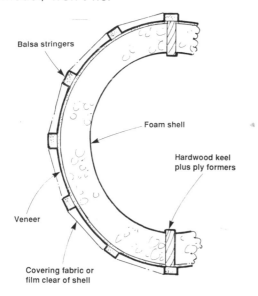

Balsa stringers

Foam shell

Hardwood keel plus ply formers

Veneer

Covering fabric or film clear of shell

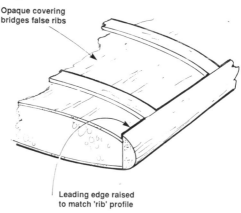

Opaque covering bridges false ribs

Leading edge raised to match 'rib' profile

Fig. 3a (left) Alternative construction for fabric-covered fuselages.
Fig. 3b (above) Add capping strips to foam/ veneer wing to simulate ribs in built-up structure.

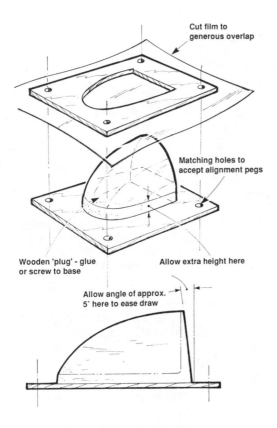

Cut film to generous overlap

Matching holes to accept alignment pegs

Wooden 'plug' - glue or screw to base

Allow extra height here

Allow angle of approx. 5° here to ease draw

Fig. 4 Plug and set-up for canopy moulding.

Composites of g.r.p. kevlar and carbon do have their uses but remember that the strength of kevlar and carbon is in tension. Any structure should be stiff enough to ensure that only the skin to be reinforced is where the additional fibres are laid. This applies to wing spars or fuselage longerons. Use it if you think you should, but since this is scale and not F3B, it is helpful but not essential.

Mould a canopy

Cockpit canopies are a frequent source of doubt among would-be scale modellers, but even a canopy for a quarter scaler should cause little problem. Time, yes, but problem, no.

We presume that a ready-made canopy for your project is not available and that it is not possible to cut a larger one down to size to suit your purpose. If this is the case, have a go at one of your own.

John Watkins' delightful K13 was built from scratch, required a large canopy moulding!

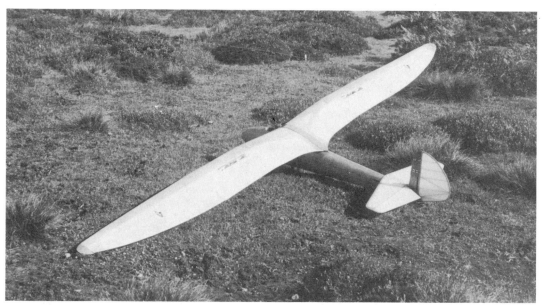

Kirby Kite IE, ¼ scale, by **Nick Somerville from John Watkins' plan. Full-size machine below.**

A P.S.S. canopy is a nice easy start and for this is needed a male mould or plug. This can be carved from one piece of, preferably, hard wood, though balsa is adequate for one-offs. Allow extra height and length over the required dimensions in order that the edge to be trimmed has some tolerance. Make up a

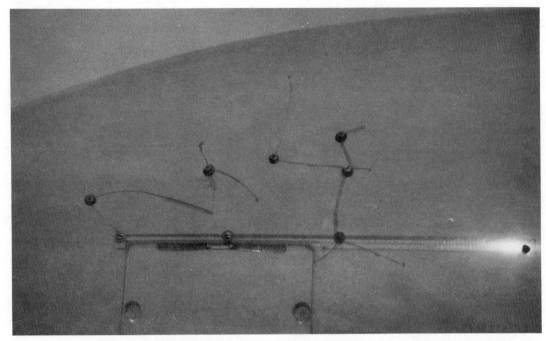

Emergency repair to stop crack spreading on full-size *K13* canopy—see text.

This nicely finished *F4E Phantom* has a "solid" canopy.

set of templates, carve and sand the block carefully. Obtain as good a finish as possible but do NOT paint or use body filler, as hot sheet will stick to most anything.

The plug should be screwed to a base board with a generous overlap and a compression plate produced as shown which will slip over the plug with an allowance for the thickness of the sheet. Drill holes for nails or metal pegs as shown to ensure that the compression plate and base will line up as the softened sheet distorts. Fig. 4 makes this clear.

We are presuming here of course that you do not have access to a vacuum forming machine—it is well worth checking amongst your pals because they can frequently be found in schools and colleges, apart from professional plastics formers for industry. The rule in my apprenticeship days was that "foreigners take precedence". Do they still? For larger canopies, the technique is very much the same though the plug construction is more involved. Basic ply templates are produced and the plug is blocked up from sheet balsa.

Remember that a moulded canopy

An *ASK 18* built and well flown by Norman Dean.

Typically, an acetate or polycarbonate film will soften at around 400°F, no. 6 on a gas oven, but it will be necessary to try a few samples before committing yourself to the final canopy.

Cut the sheet with a generous overlap, coat well with vegetable cooking oil as a release agent, set between top and bottom mould pieces and place in your preheated oven. As the sheet softens, push the compression plate evenly down until the canopy is fully formed, then remove, allow to cool and trim to suit.

invariably retains internal stresses which can be relieved by gentle warming for 10 minutes or so. Still be careful, of course, for a scratch can become a crack, and a crack a split which is difficult to repair.

A useful trick to prevent a crack from spreading is to drill a hole at the end. Any cut-outs such as for clear view panels should be carefully blended into holes drilled into each corner. Take a look at the photo which shows a temporary repair on the canopy on the K13 we were flying at Hucklow. This was the result of

The *Kite* (also shown on p.29) would not look right flying without a pilot showing.

a ground handling error, not strafing by some other sailplane . . .

Should you not really require a clear canopy, incidentally, it is adequate to carve from balsa and paint a simulated canopy as can be seen on a few P.S.S. photographs. A female mould can be produced from this in g.r.p. and used to make a g.r.p. canopy which can remain translucent or be painted in a solid

Fig. 5a Pilot proportions.

Multiply height h" by scale by factor,
ie., 72" x ¼ x 0.15 = 2.7"

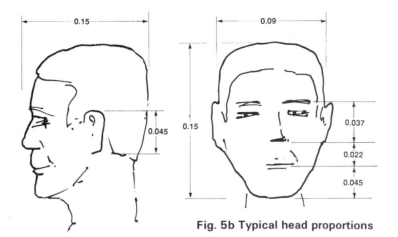

Fig. 5b Typical head proportions

colour. Pale blue or green makes a neutral to complement any aircraft. Just don't worry too much if the shape is right.

Carve a pilot?

While a canopy makes a scale model, a pilot finally sets it off and a little care and research makes it right.

Proportions of the figure in whole or part are important and the sketches give you a guide to the average human physique. Multiply the factors given by pilot's height times scale to give your dummy pilot's dimensions. Needless to say, if there is a false floor in the cockpit, the figure is cut back to suit.

Blue foam is a useful material for

Attractive pilot/cockpit details by John Elliott on his *K13*.

No shortage of space in the average ¼ scale fuselage, but a false floor would help this one.

coat. Hats, sunglasses, harnesses, clothing etc. can be added to suit—don't skimp that job.

The traditional model paints can be used for final painting, but do use matt paints in fairly neutral colours. Do not overdo the colours on the face or the result will look like a make-up ad.

Hair can be simulated with matt paint on a "combed" surface, but any attempt to add fibre to represent a thatch will almost certainly result in the appearance of a toupee. Most P.S.S. pilots will be wearing a helmet and any glider pilot would be wise to wear a hat, so this should not present too much of a problem.

Cockpit details

The instrument panel is always a worthwhile feature on a scale glider and, where possible, on a P.S.S. model. There are ways to produce a three dimensioned

An en-print photo cut out and with the background blacked out makes a very reasonable simulation of the instruments.

making a figure. "Carve" with soldering iron and clothe with lightweight tissue stuck on with PVA glue.

The head, of course, can make the supreme difference and again, proportions are all-important. There are a few ways to make realistic features. Cut a block of foam and "carve" to shape as accurately as possible. A final skin can be produced by laying on a smear of Plasticine which can be worked with scalpel and pointed stick to achieve the desired result. Paint with epoxy to seal the surface. Alternatively, use a balsa base block and build up facial features a little at a time using car body filler. Use as little hardener as possible to give plenty of setting time, for this material can be worked to as much detail as required. Carve any final details and add a skin of epoxy before the base under-

Attention to detail on Norman Dean's *ASK 18* includes maps and canopy clear-view panel.

panel but it should be adequate to use a photograph with the background painted matt black to highlight the instruments.

Other details such as cable and canopy release, lever for air brakes, trim levers etc. can be added at your discretion. Oxygen bottle etc. are great too but some of the nicest touches I have seen are a miniature chocolate bar, ordnance survey map, and a copy of "Sailplane and Gliding" down the side of the cockpit. Fine if you have the time!

Superb *Rheinland* by Brian Grace, an elegant gull-wing design typical of its day. Size of canopy means that cockpit detail is virtually essential!

Chapter 3
Deviations?

Almost every full-size aircraft will make a good P.S.S. subject and even improbable ones will, at a stretch. A little cheating on scale accuracy is acceptable providing that the finished result is a sincere attempt to make the model flyable rather than a caricature of the aircraft with sailplane proportions.

Note that on static judging some marks are given for accuracy of outline, but this may only be, say, ten percent of the possible overall maximum score, and thus any changes for flying benefits may only cost a couple of points. These may be more than made up for in the flying section, so you decide how far to go in any concessions to flying ability.

The challenge is to convince the judges that your entry is exceedingly accurate and most models are checked against a three-view drawing for profile, planform and underside proportions. A little stretching to gain area or nose moment for instance can be forgiven if this is done proportionately, i.e. increase span and chord on wing and tail, reduce fuselage height and width progressively over the length. Note that we are not advocating cheating or encouraging deviations from scale but a few percent more or less in the right place could make a difference.

While resting on the ground, a little extra span on the model is not that obvious or offensive. Choice of colour scheme of course can create an illusion of a fatter fuselage or broader chord wing. The harassed judge may not have noticed if the model was tilted back slightly to minimise the effects of stretched wing but since he will surely be generous with points for originality in choice of prototype, this chance is worth taking. The rate of taper is the critical item and should be held as closely as possible.

Control surfaces are our other main concern. Although we have control by radio, the model must still retain some inherent stability. Some wing flex may give effective dihedral but ailerons, elevator and rudder must be large enough to give guide response at model flying speeds. Non-standard sizes invariably means longer and/or wider. Again, colour schemes and markings can disguise the differences though the judges, with an understanding of the problems, are naturally more tolerant on this point.

Engine nacelles and jet pods have brought their own problems due to drag and possibilities of damage on landing. Simple knock-off fixings with internal rubber bands or Velcro are possible

This semi scale *Skylark* featuring built-up construction has increased wing area by using a slight increase in chord, particularly towards the tips.

Not to the same scale, this *Me110* and *FW190* nevertheless make an interesting pair.

No retracts and a solid canopy, but excellent work on the markings makes a most convincing model of the *Grumman A6 Invader* by **Ron Collins**.

while large pods such as those on the Lockheed A10 and Lear Jet can be represented just as a hollow shell. No one has yet fitted free wheeling propellers or fan intakes though no doubt they will in time.

A free wheeling fan could be made to simulate jet engine noise—perhaps as welcome as a machine gun sound or Stuka siren. You could set a new trend, though the last thing we want is for gliders to sound like powered aircraft! That would be intolerable.

Tolerable, however, are the other variations needed to produce a practical flying model. A retracting undercarriage is a delightful addition to a model sailplane, but fixed undercarriages are not really practicable where a heavy P.S.S. model is to be set down on our heather, gorse and rock-strewn slopes. A painted line to represent the under-carriage door is acceptable and a remov-able section with half a wheel and "opened" doors could be deceptive enough to score a few points on static judging at a scale event. (Don't tell them if they don't ask you.) There won't be any points for working features, however, so why not do the job properly?

On a P.S.S. job, opening cockpit canopies and clear view panels will not earn you extra marks any more than a swivelling gun turret, unless you can do this while flying, so we say again, put the skill into the illusion of detail finishing.

Chapter 4
Colour and markings

With the advent of colour film and quick service processing laboratories, one thing that has become apparent is that any photographs you take may not accurately reproduce the shade or perhaps even the colour of the original. Although it may hurt, it is perhaps more important that your model matches the photographs than the original and it is strongly advised that any photography done for documentation should be done with good quality film,

The only way to obtain the transparency of doped fabric is to use similar methods. This is a 1/5 scale scratch-built Polish *Komar* by Mick Moore.

Plain finish on this *Tornado* contrasts with similar model opposite.

through a quality processing laboratory and printed on matt paper. With cheap film, you get what you pay for...

Even full-sized aircraft colour schemes shown in books and magazines may not accurately depict the original aircraft, which may show the effects of a non-standard undercoat, an abrasive environ-

This *SuperSabre* is a kit for ducted fan use, but is worth looking at for conversion.

Much more elaborate *Tornado* markings enhance overall appearance.

ment or ingrained dirt from prolonged usage. Verify the colour that you wish to copy with whatever photograph or printed evidence comes to hand, then worry about how this is going to be obtained.

It is possible to mix or have mixed an accurate match to whatever colour you require, but brushing on comes a poor

Detail by decal on this fine *SuperSabre* model, not incidentally the one opposite.

second to spraying. Lots of information has been published on what is known as "air brushing", in reality a compressed air spray gun and from a purpose mixed paint, this is the only way to go. It is a cheaper alternative to aerosol car match paints for large models.

There is a seemingly infinite range of touch-up colours for car bodies and these are capable of blending and subtle variations by use of alternative under-coats. With these aerosol paints, it is essential to note that there is little or no "body" in the colour. Spray a pass over a piece of glass and you will note that the result is "translucent", that is, you can see through it. Spray on an undercoat in a different area and you will have a solid colour that is opaque; light will pass through but you cannot see through it.

Next overspray the undercoat with colour of your choice and allow to dry. Then using a piece of card to mask one third of the area, spray over again. Repeat this and compare the results. Try this experiment again using different colours of undercoat and you will begin to see the changes which can be effected in this way.

Further variations can be obtained by spraying a gloss lightly onto an under-coat, then a finishing gloss perhaps of a variation to this colour. Remember that this gloss is translucent and the final appearance will be influenced by the colour that it is sprayed over—almost the same as mixing in the can.

Careful use permits many variations on the camouflage theme, particularly where a mottled effect is required or one colour is blended into another. Masking tape, stencil or templates can be used for any other lines, patterns, letters or markings for special effects. Unfortun-

The closer you get the better the detail on John Hill's *Tucano*, **right and opposite. Spinners and prop hubs worthwhile additions.**

Simple but effective *Tomahawk* colour scheme can be achieved with brushwork.

Almost any aeroplane can be adapted for P.S.S. provided its wing area is reasonable.

Leading P.S.S.A. Figure Alan Hulme carved this *Nimrod* from blue foam.

ately, car aerosols are not a cheap way of painting a model, but they certainly are versatile, quick and convenient.

Iron-on film can be used for letters, roundels, emblems and other markings —not to mention overall covering, of course. Self adhesive trim tape lends itself to panel lines, simulated cockpit frames etc. Simply lay out a length sticky side down on glass. Use a straight edge and balsa knife to strip out to suit, peel off and stick into place. (Take off and discard any unused tape or you'll have a struggle to remove it from the glass.)

The glass and scalpel blade technique can be used to match masking tape to awkward shapes and curves. Press masking tape down firmly, then lightly overspray again with the previous colour to seal the edges and allow to set hard before applying the next colour. Progress patiently and any design can be built up. The draughtsman's ink pen has a variety of tip diameters and drawing around templates, french curves or a straight edge will give an excellent effect. Use it also for rivet marks and so on but do apply them accurately, for a freehand application will never look satisfactory.

R.M. Green with his 78in *B52* a good flier.

44

Insignia can be hand-painted quite accurately. Use model paints with a flatting agent to paint inside a line applied by carbon paper or whatever means you prefer. Allow each coat to dry fully before adding further paints and draw in the outline to each colour with the ink pen after all the paint is fully dry. A wide selection of dry fix letters and shapes is available, incidentally, check out the sheets available for industry with marks for designers and photoetching— a combination of one or more shapes could be just what you are looking for.

Obviously, the craftsman in you will no doubt wish to keep going in the application of marks and markings but, eventually, the time must come to finish off. It is not essential to reproduce the markings faithfully, remember we used the word "illusion"?

Final touches include things such as oil and exhaust stains which are not difficult to do and add real "used" character to your model—just don't overdo it. When the final result looks right, you will know and, at this stage, it will be necessary to seal the work.

Matt polyurethane or artist's aerosol spray fixative can be used to finish the project. Do be sure, though, that anything you apply will not lift or attack any of the paint or markings you have so patiently applied.

Be sure not to rush this procedure. Remember, too, that almost any aircraft you come across will have a matt surface finish. Progressive wet and dry paper will cut down highlights and flat out the paint to a good smooth finish—just don't use brazing paste or polish, unless that aircraft really did sparkle.

The Ray Jones *B52* **over the Clwyd slopes.**

Chapter 5
Launching and flying

From the slope, we tend to take launching methods for granted. The only concession normally made is when the wind is very strong and perhaps generating turbulence, in which case the launcher may take the model down the face of the hill to where the air is a little smoother. In these conditions, a large model becomes a team effort in handling with holder/chucker and one or more to steady a wing tip. Coordinate that lot!

A gentle breeze can be even more taxing, for it is necessary for the launcher to run down the slope for the model to obtain flying speed. Time and time again I have seen the launcher disappear down the hill in a flurry of arms and legs after the model. I have not seen many people launch a quarter-scaler single-handed, though this is possible by balancing the model in the palm of one hand while holding the transmitter in the other. Not easy, particularly in severe turbulence, but possible.

Many P.S.S. models are not easy to grip due to low wings, broad chords etc. and a few of us are now reverting to a short bungee to get the models away. See Figs. 6a & 6b. This is particularly helpful where indifferent lift persists. The height gained from a bungee launch at least gives one a chance to make a top landing rather than the usual trip to the bottom of the hill or a slope-side landing.

Perfect launch for this *Grunau Baby*— **straight and level and look at the height gained already.**

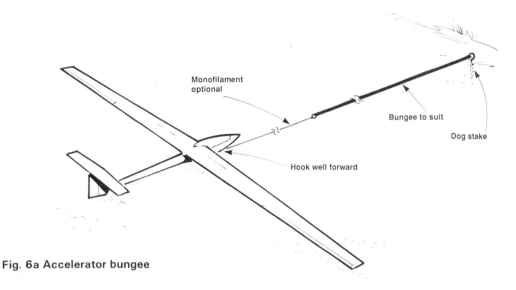

Monofilament optional

Bungee to suit

Dog stake

Hook well forward

Fig. 6a Accelerator bungee

You will need to experiment with strengths and lengths of bungee to suit the model that you intend to launch. This system is due for general adoption—full-size gliders have used it for years. An extension (if you will pardon the pun) to this system is to actually use the bungee as a catapult for the Mach 1+ type models—that will really get them away. Of course there is no reason why this could not be used from a flat field either.

The traditional bungee or towline can be used for P.S.S. or scale models when size, wing loadings and conditions permit. A useful trick, though, is to use the reverse pulley technique which will get almost anything into the air, although a power winch is even better and will solve any problems if you can get your hands on one.

Air towing is an interesting operation widely used in full-size gliding and very popular on the Continent.

The piggy back or belly launched system should also be mentioned, too. There are a number of examples of aircraft being launched from others, such as the Bell X series research craft from a B52, the Kamikaze Ohka from the Betty bomber, the Me 163 and piloted V1 experimental aircraft to name but a few

Fig. 6b Extra boost for large models.

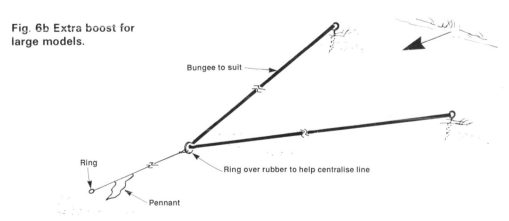

Bungee to suit

Ring

Ring over rubber to help centralise line

Pennant

The DFS230-A1 troop-carrying glider has a nice easily-gripped slab-sider fuselage.

comparatively recent examples. This is where your browsing could take you into fields anew.

Flying

At a number of scale and P.S.S. events I have attended, the lift has been poor—evidenced by the number of fliers who are to be seen climbing back up the hill after landing out. In these circumstances, height gain from a launch is invaluable. Keeping the model close in to the hill then holds the model in whatever lift there may be, permitting a top landing should there be insufficient to keep it airborne. Pushing out away from the slope has only one ending when the lift is by your kneecaps. Still, the exercise will do you good!

Local knowledge of which parts of your slope work best in certain wind directions and strengths gives a tremen-

dous advantage. Should you be flying "away from home", however, watch the locals, though do be aware that they may not know all the answers either.

The diversity of hill lift is tremendous. A stronger wind may not necessarily generate lift as it depends on contours, shapes and the terrain upwind. The gradient affects compressibility and may simply speed up the air flow without generating more lift. The only answer is to go and look for it. The lift that is!

Any rapid and significant improvement in lift is almost certain to be thermal-induced—the birds will probably be onto it before you are. Reaction will depend on where the lift is encountered. Should this be close in, then follow up and back, for the rising air will almost certainly be spilling like a waterfall in reverse over the lip of the hill. Circling in this area should provide a progressive height gain

A T21 going up on the winch.

Keep the wings level and nose down. A steadying hand at the tip is useful in strong winds.

How not to, by the author. A good heave and a gust see the *Discus* already requiring corrective action.

Balance on the right hand while steadying with the left. The launcher gallops to gain flying speed before release.

No blow, no go!
Ron Collins can still
raise a rueful smile
after a retrieval trip.

even though the model comes back to the ridge at head height. Do not be afraid to circle back going downwind—as long as the model is going up for pushing back to the ridge, it should still be flying in lift. At least a top landing will save your legs.

Thermal lift out from the ridge has probably broken and lifted some distance upwind and may well have expanded to the point where its effect is dying. Current terminology calls this "negative sink" and it is usually possible to circle round without much loss of height. At this stage, following downwind could be helpful, if only to get back to slope lift, for the axiom is "behind every thermal there is SINK". Who wants to be dumped down the hill—again?

The tendency to confuse minimum

From the bottom up.
A long slog for Roy
Cox to retrieve his
Reiher: it happens to
everyone!

Vintage models in a thermal. No prize for guessing where the centre lies!

sink and minimum flying speed must be cured too. Some aircraft will fly slowly with a very forgiving stall pattern, but an airfoil on the verge of falling out of the sky cannot be working efficiently. Learn to recognise the flying attitude of the model and the slowest speed at which handling is "comfortable" and stick to this regardless. Mark the position of the elevator trim on your transmitter if necessary. Symptoms of flying too slowly are mushing, sluggish response to control movements and a disgusting height loss as the model falls in on the turns—and this is before it actually stalls.

Keep control movements to a minimum and those turns flat so that the model will be well placed for the next thermal that comes through.

When landing, we have a slightly different problem in that any turbulence, wind shear or increase in wind speed by ground effect can slow down the model at a time when control is critical. Air is required to flow over the control surfaces to affect the flight path of a model—too slow and there is no control. An aircraft dropping the last few feet is not a pretty sight, so keep that speed a little higher than the effective minimum sink to maintain control. Literally fly the model down parallel to the ground and pop out the brakes, for if that nose comes up— you've lost.

Good lift does in fact bring its own problems, for any attempt to lose surplus height can result in the model gaining excessive speed—not easy to lose without brakes. It is an amusing contrast to fly avoiding thermal lift (like playing "takes" with a chess set) but essential where manoeuvres have to be assessed where the judges can actually see them. Always a good idea to grab the lift while it is there, though, for it is easier to shed height than to gain it. A low slow fly-by, however, is hardly realistic when streaking past with the wind whistling through the control surfaces!

Chapter 6
Fly a competition?

The business of contest flying is somewhat contradictory, for I am convinced that for the majority of entrants winning is the least important consideration. Satisfying, but not essential. There is a trend to "fly-ins" which nevertheless have winners but absolutely no losers. The traditional style of event does still take place, so let's have a look what goes on.

Over the years, scale events have evolved a widely accepted format which has been adopted in part by P.S.S. Briefly, the challenge is to choose and research a prototype, then build, detail, finish and mark accordingly. This is

Static judging from outside a fixed circle equalises cockpit and other fine detail but does not detract from the satisfaction of scale or near-scale modelling.

Up there, and a beautiful sunny day for a super scale competition.

verified by one or more judges from outside a circle 25 ft or so in diameter which means that all that wonderful cockpit detail was not really essential—apart from giving personal satisfaction.

Be there on the day well before scheduled start time, have a test flight if you really must, otherwise carefully rig your model/s and take a look around. By the time you have nattered to old friends and seen the latest offerings, briefing will be called and the tasks for the day will be announced. Pay attention or you'll have to ask someone else what to do—could you trust their sense of humour?

Humour? At this time the wind either changes direction, develops into a gale or drops altogether, the rain starts, mist comes down or any combination of these. At this time you may also remember where you left your tailplane and waterproofs, so think first, eh?

Most times, however, the weather is great and when called for static judging,

if there are working features like brakes and retracts to display, the first thing to do is grab the frequency peg, switch on transmitter (with the aerial down of course), on with the receiver, operate the controls and switch off in the reverse order. Peg and transmitter back to control first before casually placing the model in the circle and handing your documentation pack to the judges . . .

It is not usually permitted to speak to the judges though occasionally they may ask questions about the model and its prototype. Since I was once (almost) penalised for having a dummy radio aerial which was assumed to be a receiver aerial and marked down accordingly, I always take the precaution of mentioning this on handing the literature over for perusal.

When called to fly, it will usually be necessary to carry out a selection of compulsory manoeuvres followed by a further set appropriate to the original.

For scale models, these could include

Phil Sirr launches his *SE5A*. A dummy propeller hub would help the illusion.

A stretched wing plus ailerons are acceptable on this *VI* for flyability.

Below, *Bell X15*, two ch., is to be launched from the Cocker B52. Like R.M. Green's *SR71A Blackbird*, sailplane proportions they haven't, and they fly accordingly.

This trio of *Vulcans* would require their speeds matched for formation flying.

straight ahead stall and recovery, stall turn, low pass demonstrating working features like brakes, retracts, flaps etc., thermal turns and so on. Freestyle choice may include aerobatics if the original was so rated. Before each manoeuvre, say what you are about to attempt, call "Begin" and "Complete" clearly and on to the next one.

This section is concluded by a judged approach and landing which in tradition is defined as "square". First a pass across wind, turn through 90° downwind, 90° across wind, then turn on approach to land. At the start of each leg, call out, "Cross-wind", "Downwind", "Base leg" and "Finals".

Points are gained for realism, smooth execution and continuity and these are added to accuracy, colour markings, detail and working feature marks to give an aggregate for the final score. Whatever scores are awarded, it is strongly advised that one never disputes any decision, though now I think about it, I can't ever remember any scale flier ever doing that...

The choice of prototype and originality may influence scores and a 'K' (constant) factor is frequently applied to penalise the entrant who chooses a kit in which the model is prefabricated. Scratch-built models also score higher than those from plans by others. Complexity also is rightly or wrongly appreciated highly and models of Vintage gliders frequently score highest in these events.

A further section in a scale event may include a cross-country in which the model must pass behind marked turn points around a course, perhaps followed by a further landing which may also be in a marked area. Manoeuvres may be specified at one or more turn points such as loops or 360° turns downwind.

The cross-country flight does not usually contribute significantly to the overall score but does give more stick time and a little extra challenge.

Power scale soarers have potentially more variety both in detail and flying. There is an infinite variety of types, colours and markings. Details including lights, guns, retracting undercarriages, flaps, and whatever are complemented by bomb, rocket, parachute and tip tank drops, smoke trails, formation flying and dog-fights. The possibilities are endless and we are looking forward to seeing a pair of Pitts Special in action or some day maybe a Red Arrows squadron formation of Hawks...

It is perhaps because of the difficulties of assessing the diverse elements on an equal basis that the 'fly-in' type of event has grown to its present day level of popularity. Certainly all the current proponents of P.S.S. delight in displaying their ingenuity.

At the end of the event, the scores are tallied and the silverware is handed out. To the winners goes admiration and a special sort of satisfaction—everyone else seems equally happy, just to have been there.

Why not give it a try?

Chapter 7
If I only had time . . .

That is a common complaint. We talk blissfully about research, designing and building scale models as though this were the easiest thing in the world. Well, it is not too difficult, does not require any special tools or facilities and depending on your means or inclinations may not be too time-consuming.

Lists of plans are available to members of the Power Scale Soaring Association and others for P.S.S. and scale are advertised and listed by various manufacturers. There is plenty of help handy, though, should you tackle your own project.

As an alternative to the scratch-built approach, there are numerous kits available, with varying degrees of prefabrication, for both scale and P.S.S.

At first sight, the cost of a typical scale kit may seem expensive, that is until one considers the amount of time that can be saved this way. Consider the equivalent hourly rate that your employer has to pay you or which you would have to pay any other skilled tradesman and the value of a kit becomes clearer. It largely depends on the reasons why the project is to be tackled in the first place.

There must be innumerable projects that are collecting dust which, had there been a set of components to hand with a sequence of instructions, would have progressed at a gallop, putting the model in the air quickly and making more time for living. Well, flying: it's the same thing . . .

One of the Horten flying wings of the 1930s and 1940s would make an interesting subject for research?

Unusual choice of P.S.S. subject is this *MiG25 Foxbat.*

Other items which do take time and do not justify the effort are such as airbrakes and retracting undercarriages. These and numerous other ready-made components and accessories are available, permitting time-saving and enabling the model of your choice to appear with a professional appearance in the minimum of time.

The attitude to purchasing odd items is a little confusing at times. It is acceptable to buy radio equipment and fittings, quick links and the like are natural to buy, yet people will work all week-end to make some other item that could have been bought for a small sum at their local model shop.

Consult magazine advertisements for details of kits and catalogues. The industry is already in a position to supply you with most things that you need, as except in rare instances it's all been done before. Get with it and save flying time.

V-tail constant-chord *Bryan HP14* **variant based at Chipping, Preston, cries out to be modelled!**

Appendix 1 – Examples of aerofoils old and new

R.A.F. 32

EPPLER 374

R.A.F. 32 / Clark Y

Chord Station	Upper Surface	Chord Station	Lower Surface	Chord Station	Upper Surface	Chord Station	Lower Surface
XU	YU	XL	YL	XU	YU	XL	YL
.000	3.420	.000	3.420	.000	3.500	.000	3.500
.200	4.200	.200	2.800	.200	4.260	.200	2.920
.400	4.550	.400	2.560	.400	4.610	.400	2.620
.600	4.870	.600	2.400	.800	5.090	.800	2.250
.800	5.140	.800	2.200	1.250	5.550	1.250	1.960
1.250	5.560	1.250	1.960	2.500	6.500	2.500	1.470
2.500	6.520	2.500	1.500	5.000	7.900	5.000	.930
5.000	7.840	5.000	.880	7.500	8.850	7.500	.630
10.000	9.720	10.000	.300	10.000	9.600	10.000	.420
15.000	11.020	15.000	.080	15.000	10.680	15.000	.150
20.000	11.920	20.000	.000	20.000	11.360	20.000	.030
30.000	12.980	30.000	.300	25.000	11.600	25.000	.000
40.000	13.100	40.000	.700	30.000	11.700	30.000	.000
50.000	12.460	50.000	1.100	40.000	11.400	40.000	.000
60.000	11.060	60.000	1.460	50.000	10.520	50.000	.000
70.000	9.100	70.000	1.600	60.000	9.150	60.000	.000
80.000	6.650	80.000	1.460	70.000	7.350	70.000	.000
90.000	3.600	90.000	.920	80.000	5.220	80.000	.000
95.000	1.980	95.000	.520	90.000	2.800	90.000	.000
100.000	.120	100.000	.120	100.000	.120	100.000	.000

(Left block: R.A.F. 32. Right block: Clark Y — For 30 percent flap)

Eppler 374 / Wortmann FX 60-126 Camber 3.6 Percent

Chord Station	Upper Surface	Chord Station	Lower Surface	Chord Station	Upper Surface	Chord Station	Lower Surface
XU	YU	XL	YL	XU	YU	XL	YL
.000	.000	.000	.000	.000	.000	.000	.000
1.250	1.400	1.250	-1.100	.102	.675	.102	-.301
2.500	2.200	2.500	-1.500	.422	1.349	.422	-.641
5.000	3.400	5.000	-2.000	.960	2.096	.960	-1.012
7.500	4.200	7.500	-2.400	1.702	2.802	1.702	-1.404
10.000	4.900	10.000	-2.700	2.650	3.493	2.650	-1.792
15.000	5.900	15.000	-3.000	3.802	4.174	3.802	-2.132
20.000	6.600	20.000	-3.100	5.158	4.808	5.158	-2.482
25.000	7.200	25.000	-3.200	6.694	5.457	6.694	-2.761
30.000	7.500	30.000	-3.300	8.422	6.021	8.422	-3.045
40.000	7.700	40.000	-3.200	10.330	6.585	10.330	-3.262
50.000	7.100	50.000	-2.900	12.403	7.077	12.403	-3.465
60.000	6.000	60.000	-2.600	14.643	7.555	14.643	-3.598
70.000	4.600	70.000	-2.200	17.037	7.958	17.037	-3.707
80.000	3.100	80.000	-1.500	19.558	8.327	19.558	-3.746
90.000	1.600	90.000	-.800	22.221	8.615	22.221	-3.751
95.000	.900	95.000	-.400	24.998	8.859	24.998	-3.683
100.000	.000	100.000	.000	27.891	9.019	27.891	-3.574
				30.861	9.130	30.861	-3.392
				33.933	9.160	33.933	-3.167
				37.056	9.138	37.056	-2.877
				40.243	9.041	40.243	-2.553
				43.469	8.893	43.469	-2.188
				46.733	8.679	46.733	-1.814
				49.997	8.425	49.997	-1.421
				53.274	8.118	53.274	-1.036
				56.525	7.781	56.525	-.653
				59.750	7.402	59.750	-.298
				62.938	6.994	62.938	.029
				66.074	6.549	66.074	.307
				69.133	6.082	69.133	.547
				72.115	5.589	72.115	.741
				74.995	5.084	74.995	.897
				77.773	4.567	77.773	1.006
				80.435	4.055	80.435	1.073
				82.970	3.552	82.970	1.093
				87.590	2.611	87.590	1.022
				89.644	2.181	89.644	.944
				91.571	1.777	91.571	.845
				93.299	1.412	93.299	.732
				94.848	1.084	94.848	.610
				96.192	.798	96.192	.483
				97.344	.554	97.344	.357
				98.291	.353	98.291	.239
				99.034	.198	99.034	.146
				99.571	.088	99.571	.068
				99.891	.024	99.891	.014
				100.000	.000	100.000	.000

(Left block: Eppler 374. Right block: Wortmann FX 60-126 — Camber 3.6 Percent)

CLARK Y

Wortmann FX 60-1261

Chord Station XU	Upper Surface YU	Chord Station XL	Lower Surface YL
.000	.000	.000	.000
.102	.359	.102	-.472
.422	1.279	.422	-.675
.960	2.086	.960	-.983
1.702	2.856	1.702	-1.308
2.650	3.545	2.650	-1.710
3.802	4.307	3.802	-2.017
5.158	4.962	5.158	-2.342
6.694	5.636	6.694	-2.594
8.422	6.224	8.422	-2.852
10.330	6.815	10.330	-3.042
12.403	7.331	12.403	-3.220
14.643	7.835	14.643	-3.327
17.037	8.260	17.037	-3.412
19.558	8.653	19.558	-3.426
22.221	8.962	22.221	-3.409
24.998	9.227	24.998	-3.319
27.891	9.405	27.891	-3.191
30.861	9.533	30.861	-2.992
33.933	9.577	33.933	-2.752
37.056	9.567	37.056	-2.449
40.243	9.478	40.243	-2.117
43.469	9.337	43.469	-1.746
46.733	9.122	46.733	-1.371
49.997	8.862	49.997	-.985
53.274	8.542	53.274	-.614
56.525	8.183	56.525	-.253
59.750	7.774	59.750	.072
62.938	7.334	62.938	.365
66.074	6.854	66.074	.609
69.133	6.354	69.133	.815
72.115	5.829	72.115	.978
74.995	5.295	74.995	1.106
77.773	4.759	77.773	1.190
80.435	4.237	80.435	1.236
82.970	3.739	82.970	1.239
87.590	2.830	87.590	1.146
89.644	2.427	89.644	1.060
91.571	2.054	91.571	.955
93.299	1.707	93.299	.836
94.848	.1381	94.848	.706
96.192	1.072	96.192	.568
97.344	.784	97.344	.427
98.291	.528	98.291	.292
99.034	.323	99.034	.182
99.571	.161	99.571	.089
99.891	.052	99.891	.021
100.000	.000	100.000	.000

WORTMANN FX 60-1261

EPPLER 193 AERODYNAMIC ZERO -3.39 DEGREES

Eppler 193 Aerodynamic Zero -3.39 degrees

Chord Station XU	Upper Surface YU	Chord Station XL	Lower Surface YL
.000	.000	.000	.000
.026	.190	.129	-.375
.465	.915	.819	-.838
1.344	1.740	2.044	-1.252
2.652	2.608	3.791	-1.588
4.383	3.487	6.049	-1.841
6.525	4.352	8.801	-2.010
9.061	5.181	12.026	-2.098
11.967	5.957	15.697	-2.112
15.218	6.663	19.778	-2.061
18.780	7.284	24.227	-1.955
22.620	7.805	28.998	-1.807
26.696	8.213	34.035	-1.628
30.967	8.487	39.280	-1.430
35.402	8.603	44.672	-1.244
39.979	8.551	50.145	-1.019
44.673	8.332	55.630	-.824
49.458	7.954	61.059	-.645
54.306	7.436	66.384	-.486
59.186	6.808	71.479	-.350
64.052	6.112	76.339	-.239
68.839	5.381	80.882	-.153
73.484	4.642	85.050	-.091
77.923	3.914	88.788	-.048
82.096	3.214	92.048	-.018
85.945	2.558	94.794	.010
89.414	1.957	97.003	.032
92.452	1.415	98.640	.034
95.023	.932	99.655	.014
97.108	.522	100.000	.000
98.674	.220		
99.661	.051		
100.000	.000		

WORTMANN FX 60-126 CAMBER 3.6 PERCENT

EPPLER 205 — PROFIL E 205 10.48%

N	X	Y	N	X	Y
0	100.000	0.000	29	1.097	1.589
1	99.655	.039	30	.331	.766
2	98.649	.174	31	.002	.055
3	97.049	.427	32	.233	-.506
4	94.916	.778	33	1.065	-.988
5	92.285	1.196	34	2.419	-1.420
6	89.175	1.668	35	4.291	-1.776
7	85.624	2.199	36	6.669	-2.053
8	81.684	2.786	37	9.534	-2.252
9	77.412	3.419	38	12.864	-2.378
10	72.866	4.088	39	16.627	-2.436
11	68.108	4.777	40	20.783	-2.435
12	63.204	5.470	41	25.290	-2.384
13	58.218	6.147	42	30.097	-2.292
14	53.217	6.782	43	35.149	-2.168
15	48.265	7.342	44	40.388	-2.021
16	43.410	7.785	45	45.751	-1.859
17	38.680	8.081	46	51.174	-1.689
18	34.101	8.214	47	56.591	-1.516
19	29.699	8.177	48	61.938	-1.345
20	25.496	7.970	49	67.149	-1.180
21	21.508	7.606	50	72.160	-1.023
22	17.764	7.111	51	76.911	-.876
23	14.302	6.507	52	81.343	-.740
24	11.157	5.811	53	85.400	-.614
25	8.360	5.040	54	89.034	-.380
26	5.937	4.211	55	92.195	-.380
27	3.909	3.344	56	94.860	-.252
28	2.292	2.461	57	97.017	-.125
			58	98.635	-.036
			59	99.651	-.003
			60	100.000	.000

$CM = -.0460$ $\beta = 2.37°$

Appendix 2 – Plans and kits for P.S.S.

AIRCRAFT	SPAN	WEIGHT (lbs)	PLAN (P) KIT (K)	SUPPLIER
BAC Jet Provost	52″	3	P	John Stewart, 63 Mount View, Roslin, Midlothian EH25 9NZ
Avro Vulcan	50″	2	P	A.S.P. Ltd, P.O. Box 35, Wolsey House, Wolsey Road, Hemel Hempstead, Herts, HP2 4SS
BAC Hawk	46″	2½	P	R.A. Conway, 51 The Glebe, Kirkliston, Scotland, EH29 9AT
BAC Hawk F1/200	56″	3½–4	P	
Aero L39 Albatross	56″	3½–4	P	
Douglas A4 Skyhawk	42″	3–3½	P	
B.A. Tornado	60″	4½–5	P	
N.A. F86 Sabre	50″	3	P	R. G. Collins, 22 Learmouth Grove, Edinburgh, EH4 1BW
Gloster Meteor	52″	3	P	
Vought Corsair	54″	3–3½	P	
H.S. Harrier GR3	48″	2¾	P	R.M. Green, 57A Long Lane, Newtown, Great Wyrley, Walsall, West Midlands, WS6 6AT
Lockheed SR81 Blackbird	57″			
	36″	2½	P	
BAC Hawk 200	47″	2½	P	
BAC Lightning Mk3	37″	1¾	P	
McDonnell F4 Phantom	48″	2¾	P	
Panavia Tornado	52″	2¾	P	
Boeing B52G	78″			
Spitfire 22	43″	2½–3	P	J.A. Hulme, 52 Mount Way, Waverton, Chester, CH3 7QF
N.A. Mustang P51B	44″	2½–3	P	
Focke Wulf TA 152H	66″	3–3½	P	
Kawasaki Hien (Tony)	46″	2½–3	P	
Hawker Hunter	38″	3	K	Flair Products, Holdscroft Wks., Blunsdon, Swindon, SN2 4AH
BAC Lightning	39″	3	K	
McDonnell F4 Phantom	31″	1¼	K	Howard Metcalfe, Brook Cott. Section, Wintershill, Durley, Southampton, SO3 2AH
Focke-Wulf 152H	51″	1¾	K	
Lockheed U2R	78″	3–3½	K	Chart Micro Mold, Station Road, East Preston, Littlehampton, West Sussex, BN16 3AG
De Havilland Vampire	50″	?	K	Pat French Models, 22 Bridge Street, Northampton, NN1 1NW
Fouga Magister	72″	4½	K	Dragon Models, 208Q Redwither Complex, Wrexham Industrial Est., Wrexham, Clwyd, LL13 9UM
Aermacchi	68″	4	K	
F 101B Voodoo	?	?		D.B. Models, 3 East Street, Irchester, Wellingborough, Northants NN9 7BG
Gates Learjet	66″	4½–5	K	Skytime soarers, (Simon Cocker), 67 Peel Street, Macclesfield, Cheshire SK11 8BL
Grumman F20 Tigershark	?	?	P	
Boeing B52 Stratofortress	106″	8½	K	
Spitfire 14/19	69″			Brian Taylor, 26 Ashcroft, Chard, Somerset, TA20 2JH
N.A. Mustang B or D	61″			
M.E. 109	61″			
M.E.110	71″			
Curtiss P40E Kittyhawk	65″			
Hawker Hurricane	65″			
D.H. Mosquito FB6	71″			
Bell Airacobra	59″	MW2121		R/C Model World, Plans Service, Masefield House, Wells Road, Malvern, Worcestershire, WR14 4PA
Fairey Firefly	61″	MW2118		
Handley Page Harrow	60″	MW2124		
M.E. 163B Komet	44″	MW2021		
Dornier 215	66″	MW2040		
Supermarine Spiteful	52″	MW2052		
Avro Vulcan	60″	MW2116		
Spitfire F22/24	56″	MW2053		
Junkers JU 52	71″	MW2070		
F15 Eagle	46″	MW2126 Ap '87		
MiG 25	36″	MW2127 Ap '87		
NA A-5A Vigilante	41″	MW2142 Sep '87		
Avro Lancaster	90″	RC1457		A.S.P. Ltd, P.O. Box 35, Wolsey House, Wolsey Road, Hemel Hempstead, Herts HP2 4SS
Avro Lancaster	74″	RM333		
Kawasaki Hien (Tony)	68″			
Lockheed P38	66″	A560		M.R.A. 12 Rue Mulet, 69001, Lyon, France.
Dewoitine 520	63″	447		
Hawker Hunter	54″	640		
Mirage 2000	43″	600		
Fiat G91	38″	165		
Morane Saulnier 406	74″	539		

Note that the above plans by Model Reduit D'avion, (M.R.A.) are available in the U.K. from – Kip Marketing, 33 Yorke Gardens, Reigate, RH2 9HQ

Appendix 3 – Useful addresses

Vintage Gliding Club
Robin Traves, Rose View, Marden Rd,
Staplehurst, Kent TN12 0JG

British Gliding Association
Kimberley House, Vaughan Way,
Leicester LE1 4SE

Power Scale Soaring Association
Alan Hulme, 52 Mountway, Waverton,
Chester CH3 7QF

*British Association of Radio Control
Soarers*
Alan Cooper, Hillcrest, Top Rd,
Wingerworth, Chesterfield, Derbyshire
S42 6RQ

*British Model Flying Federation
(formerly SMAE)*
Kimberley House, Vaughan Way,
Leicester LE1 4SE

Civil Aviation Authority
Aviation House, South Area, Gatwick
Airport, West Sussex RH6 0YR

Vintage Sailplane Association
Scott Airpark, Lovettsville, Virgina USA
22082

Soaring Society of America
PO Box E, Hobbs, New Mexico, USA
88241-1308

Bibliography

references with very useful drawings
and photographs

*The World's Vintage Sailplanes 1908–
45* – Martin Simons (1986)
Kookaburra Technical Publications Pty
Ltd., Melbourne

*Janes World of Sailplanes and Motor
Gliders* – Andrew Coates (1978)
Macdonalds and Jane's, London

Segelflugzeuge 1935–1985 –
Peter E Selinger (1986) Motorbuch
Verlag, Stuttgart

Die Beruhmtesten Segelflugzeuge –
George Brutting (1977) Motorbuch
Verlag, Stuttgart

Die Segelflugzeuge in Deutschlande –
Dietmar Geistmann (1979) Motorbuch
Verlag, Stuttgart

*Die Entwicklung der Kunstoft
Segelflugzeuge* – Dietmar Geistmann
(1980) Motorbuch Verlag, Stuttgart

Appendix 4 – Example of informal competition form and note on model restrictions

The form at right, used by Wolverhampton club, is self-explanatory and is typical of 'fly-in' type competitions.

Model restrictions

There may be certain restrictions to the flying of 'heavy' radio control model aircraft in some countries, requiring special exemptions from the aviation governing bodies. For example, in the U.K. any radio control model aircraft weighing more than 5kg in a ready to fly state requires an exemption certificate, which dictates certain conditions. These may include a complete ban in controlled air space without specific permission from the appropriate air traffic control unit, a height limit of perhaps 400ft. above ground level, restrictions on distance from operator (500m or visual range, whichever is less) and in distance from buildings and vehicles; a working fail-safe device is also likely to be required. At the time of printing negotiations were taking place on possible amendments to the Air Navigation Order relating to 'Large models'. Exemption certificates in the U.K. are obtained from the Civil Aviation Authority.

C — COMPETITION

NAME		FLIGHT NUMBER
MODEL		
FREQ		

MODEL TYPE	RING SCORE
SCRATCH BUILT	40
BUILT FROM COMML PLAN	30
BUILT FROM KIT	20
BOUGHT READY MADE	10
/////////////////////	MARK OUT OF 40
COMPLEXITY	
ACCURACY OF OUTLINE	
ACCURACY OF COLOUR	
TOTAL STATIC MARK MAX 160	

MANOEUVRES (2 STATIONS)	1 FLIGHT SCORE	2 FLIGHT SCORE
LEFT TURNS MAX 100 MARKS ENTER EXIT STATION 1		
FIGURE 8 MAX. 100 MARKS STATION 1		
STALL TURN MAX. 100 MARKS STATION 2		
STATION 2	MAX 300	MAX 300
CLIMBING TURN TO RIGHT (MAX 100) 3 THERMAL TURNS TO THE LEFT (MAX 100) DESCEND STRAIGHT & LEVEL 2 DIRECTIONS ALONG SLOPE (MAX 100)		
TURN POINT 1 TICK WITH FELT MARKER	100	100
TURN POINT 2 TICK WITH FELT MARKER	100	100
APPROACH & LANDING (NO OVERSHOOT) 50 100 50 MARK APPROACH OUT OF 100 + LANDING SCORE	MAX 200	MAX 200
TOTAL FLIGHT MARK MAX 1000		
TOTAL STATIC MARK MAX 160		
TOTAL STATIC + BOTH FLIGHTS MAX 2160		

Appendix 5 – Examples of possible P.S.S. subjects

Macchi MB.326

DRAWN BY IAN R STAIR
TRACED BY A A P LLOYD

Colour code
A – Aluminium; **B** – Black; **FO** – Fluorescent orange; **G** – Green; **LG** – Light grey; **MB** – Matt Black; **ME** – Medium earth; **MG** – Medium green; **R** – Red; **W** – White. Note that red band on fuselage and black bands on wings and fuselage are 1⅝in wide.

5 = 2.1/4" × 3" W. with B. edge
6 = 3.1/2 × 3¼ B
7 = 3.1/2" × 3" W. with B. edge and square
8 = 3.1/4" × 3.1/4" B. (W. on tip tanks)
------ = small lettering 1/2" high
9 = W (B. on some light coloured aircraft)

Scale
0 1 2 3 4 5 6 7 8 ft
0 1 2m

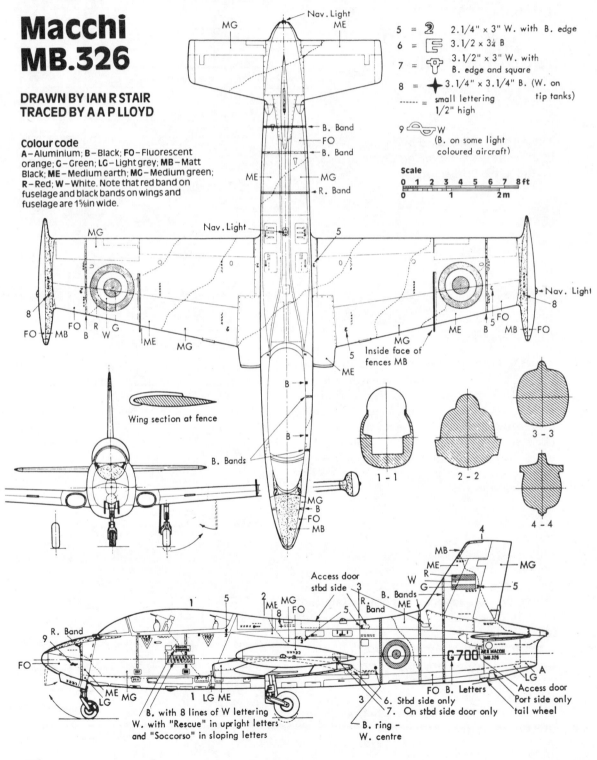

Wing section at fence

Inside face of fences MB

1 – 1   2 – 2   3 – 3   4 – 4

B. with 8 lines of W lettering W. with "Rescue" in upright letters and "Soccorso" in sloping letters

6. Stbd side only
7. On stbd side door only

Access door stbd side

B. ring – W. centre

Access door Port side only tail wheel

FO B. Letters

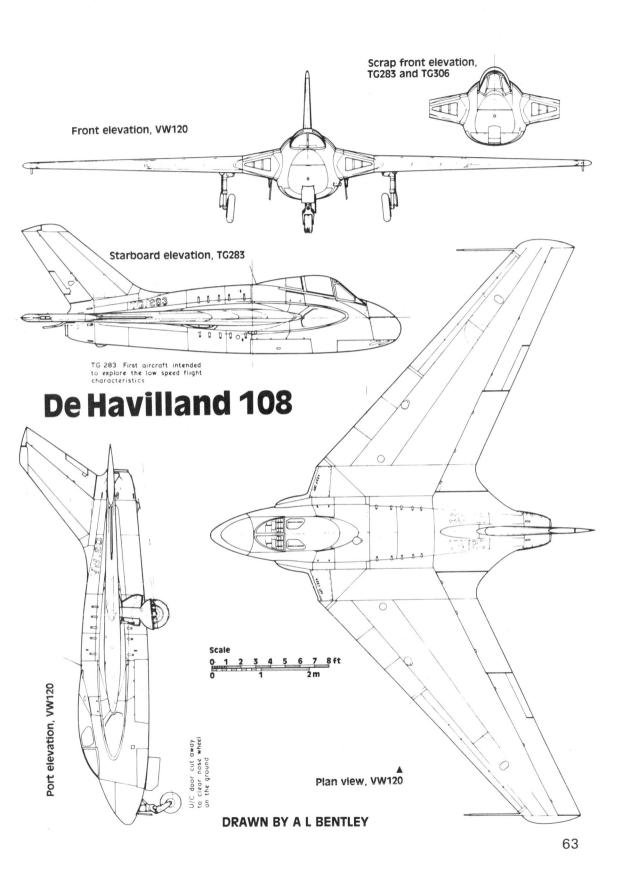

Scrap front elevation,
TG283 and TG306

Front elevation, VW120

Starboard elevation, TG283

TG 283 First aircraft intended
to explore the low speed flight
characteristics

De Havilland 108

Port elevation, VW120

U/C door cut away
to clear nose wheel
on the ground

Scale

0 1 2 3 4 5 6 7 8 ft

0   1   2 m

Plan view, VW120

DRAWN BY A L BENTLEY